CHINA TRAVEL (
2023

Uncover The Hidden Gems of China:
The Ultimate Travel Guide to
Discover the Rich Culture, Stunning
Landscapes, 10 Top Attractions, a

James J Johnson

TABLE OF CONTENTS

My Vacation In China

I arrived at Beijing Capital International Airport on a lovely June day, eager to start my holiday in China. The strong sunlight highlighted the busy streets as the air was heavy with humidity. The contrast between the historic architecture and the contemporary infrastructure that flanked the streets was what first caught my attention.

I proceeded to my hotel, which was in the center of the city, after clearing customs. The sights, sounds, and aromas of China enveloped me as I strolled through the streets. A distinctive and lively environment was produced by the combination of the smell of street food, the hum of traffic, and the talk of residents.

The Forbidden City, a large palace complex that served as the residence of the Chinese emperors for many years, was my first trip. I was astounded by the buildings' sheer size and majesty when I entered the gates. The elaborate roofing and dexterous carvings were evidence of the artistry and skill of the ancient Chinese artists.

I walked around the palace all day, admiring the splendor of the gardens and the grandeur of the royal throne chamber. I also spent time reading up on the Forbidden City's history and its significance in Chinese culture.

The following day, I went to see the Great Wall of China, one of the most recognizable structures on the planet. I was astounded by the wall's immense size and beauty as it spanned miles across the untamed terrain. I spent several hours hiking around the wall, admiring the amazing vistas of the surroundings.

I went into the city in the evenings to discover the local culture. I tried some authentic Chinese food, such as Peking duck and spicier Szechuan dishes. Additionally, I went to a nearby teahouse where I learned about the intricate aspects of Chinese tea culture and had the chance to try some of the best teas on the planet.

My trip's highlight was a trip to Xi'an's renowned Terracotta Warriors. Farmers stumbled into this ancient army of life-sized clay soldiers in the 1970s, and today it is a UNESCO World Heritage Site. I spent hours roaming through the site, admiring the creativity and craftsmanship of the old artists, who had created thousands of beautiful statues.

I also used the chance to go see Chengdu's famous pandas, which are regarded as a national treasure in China. It was so much fun to watch these cute creatures play and connect. I became aware of the conservation initiatives being taken to safeguard these threatened species, and I was moved by the commitment and consideration shown by the research center workers.

I was amazed by the friendliness and hospitality of the Chinese people throughout my entire journey. I was able to converse with people and establish new acquaintances despite the language barrier. I also seized the chance to brush up on my knowledge of traditional Chinese medicine, calligraphy, and paper cutting.

I thought back on the amazing experiences I had in China as my journey came to an end. I was appreciative of the chance to travel throughout this lovely and diverse nation and discover more about its fascinating history and culture. From the grand palaces to the modest teahouses, China had captured my heart and given me experiences I would treasure forever.

Introduction:

China is the most populous nation in the world, and it has a lengthy and rich cultural history. It is a nation with a varied geography, ranging from the tropical beaches of Hainan Island to the snow-capped Himalayan peaks. With a rich regard for tradition and culture, it has a long history of dynasties and empires.

Customs and Culture:

China's lengthy and complicated past has influenced its distinctive and diversified culture. The Chinese are renowned for their warmth, friendliness, and love of art, literature, and food. Many traditional performances from China's long history of music, dance, and theater are still put on today. The Chinese language, which has a large vocabulary and a distinctive writing system, is also one of the oldest and most difficult languages in the world.

Chinese culture has a strong foundation in tradition and reverence for the elderly and family. Additionally, respect for authority is a significant component of Chinese culture. When introducing themselves, people frequently bow, and young people frequently show respect for older persons in social settings.

Ideal Season to Visit:

Depending on where you want to go and what you want to see, there is no one optimal time to visit China. China has a variety of climates, ranging from a frigid, dry north to a balmy, tropical south. The summer months of June through August are when most tourists travel, but it may also be the hottest and busiest time of year during this time.

Since the weather is mild and there are fewer tourists, spring and autumn are typically regarded as the ideal seasons to travel. In many regions of the nation, the fall foliage is equally breathtaking, with vivid shades of red, yellow, and gold.

Travel and visa prerequisites:

A visa is typically required for entry into China for tourists. Whether a visit is for business, pleasure, or education will determine the type of visa needed. Visas can be obtained from a visa service or the Chinese embassy or consulate in your native country.

Additionally, tourists should be aware of China's stringent entrance rules, which might include medical examinations, quarantine periods, and limitations on specific foods and medications. Before making travel arrangements to China, it is crucial to review the most recent travel warnings and entrance criteria.

Money and Exchange of Currencies:

The Chinese Yuan (CNY), often called the Renminbi (RMB), is the official unit of currency in China. Before traveling to China, it is advisable to exchange money because it might be challenging to locate banks or ATMs that accept international cards.

In larger towns and tourist destinations, credit cards are accepted, but cash is still frequently preferred as a form of payment. Additionally, it's a good idea to keep little amounts and spare change on hand since many locations might not be able to exchange larger bills.

How to Travel to China:

High-speed trains, local buses, and taxis are just a few of the alternatives available in China's extensive and effective transportation network. The nation has a vast network of roads, railroads, and bus terminals that are all of the most recent designs.

With trains capable of reaching speeds of up to 350 km/h, the high-speed train network is one of the most well-liked ways to travel between large cities. In most places, buses and taxis are also easily accessible, and many cities have bike-sharing programs as well.

China is a fascinating, intricate nation with a vibrant past and present. Friendly locals will extend a warm welcome to guests and provide a variety of experiences, including touring historic temples and landmarks and taking in contemporary cuisine and entertainment. A vacation to China can be a fascinating and rewarding experience with careful planning and research.

Chapter 1:Top 10 Attractions

The Chinese Great Wall:

One of the most well-known sites in the world is the Great Wall of China, which is situated in that country. This wall is a collection of fortifications that were constructed over several centuries, starting in the 7th century BC. One of the few man-made constructions that can be viewed from space, the wall runs for more than 13,000 kilometers.

China's Great Wall was erected as a defense against invasion by nearby tribes and nations. Due to its ability to facilitate the transportation of commodities between various parts of China, it was also employed as a commerce route. Millions of visitors visit the wall every year as one of China's most well-known tourist destinations nowadays.

China's Forbidden City

In the center of Beijing, China, there lies a sizable palace complex called the Forbidden City. One of the best-preserved imperial palaces in the world, it served as the residence of the Chinese emperors for more than 500 years. The Forbidden City, which has more than 980 buildings and 8,000 rooms, was constructed during the Ming era. The Outer Court and the Inner Court are the two main areas of the palace complex, which is bounded by a moat and a high wall. The emperor and his family lived in the Inner Court, while the Outer Court was utilized for ceremonial purposes. The Forbidden City is now a museum that the general public is welcome to visit.

Xi'an's Terracotta Army

The Terracotta Army is a group of terracotta statues that were interred alongside Qin Shi Huang, the first emperor of China, in 210–209 BC. In 1974, farmers in Xi'an, China, who were excavating a well, stumbled upon the sculptures. The Terracotta Army is one of the most visited tourist destinations in China and is now a UNESCO World Heritage site.

More than 8,000 life-size sculptures of soldiers, horses, chariots, and other figures make up the Terracotta Army. The statues were made to guard the emperor in the afterlife, and they are organized in a pattern reminiscent of an ancient Chinese army.

The Shanghai Bund:

Shanghai, China's The Bund is a storied waterfront district. Its location along the Huangpu River and its stunning views of the skyline make it famous. The Bund was formerly the hub of global trade and finance. It was built in the late 19th century when China was still a colony.

The Oriental Pearl Tower and the Shanghai Tower are two of Shanghai's most recognizable structures, and the Bund is now a well-liked tourist destination. The region is also well-known for its upscale dining and retail options as well as for its vibrant nightlife.

The Guilin's Li River

In Guilin, China, there is a beautiful river called the Li River. It is renowned for its stunning karst scenery, which includes high limestone cliffs and azure water. Boat cruises along the Li River are very well-liked and provide breathtaking views of the surroundings.

There are several tiny towns and villages along the Li River where tourists can get a taste of the customs and culture of the area. The region is renowned for the production of rice, tea, and other agricultural products as well as for its traditional fishing methods.

Giant panda breeding research center in Chengdu, China: The Chengdu Research Base of Giant Panda Breeding is a research center. To preserve and breed giant pandas, an endangered species, it was founded in 1987. One of Chengdu's most well-liked tourist destinations, the base is home to more than 100 pandas.

Visitors can see pandas in their natural surroundings at the Chengdu Research Base and learn about the breeding and conservation programs being used to keep these famous animals safe. Additionally, there is a panda kindergarten within the establishment where guests can observe young pandas up close and watch them play.

Base Camp for Mount Everest:

The highest peak in the world, Mount Everest, is situated in the Himalayas between China and Nepal. Climbers and tourists alike like visiting the base camp on the mountain's Chinese side. Only through trekking is it possible to reach the base camp, which is situated at an altitude of 5,200 meters (17,060 feet).

Although getting to base camp is difficult, the views of the mountain and its neighboring peaks are breathtaking. Due to the base camp's location in an area with a significant Tibetan population, visitors can also get a taste of the native Tibetan way of life.

Lhasa's Potala Palace:

In Lhasa, Tibet, there is a sizable palace complex called the Potala Palace. One of Tibet's most significant cultural and historical sites, it was previously the residence of the Dalai Lama, the country's spiritual leader.

The palace, which has 13 floors and more than 1,000 chambers, was constructed in the seventh century. It is embellished with exquisite sculptures and artwork and serves as a reminder of Tibet's rich cultural past. The Potala Palace is now a museum and a well-liked tourist destination that draws people from all over the world to admire its beauty and significance.

Huangshan's Yellow Mountains

In China's Anhui province, there is a mountain range known as the Yellow Mountains or Huangshan. Their majestic peaks, wide valleys, and picturesque panoramas are well-known. The mountains are regarded as one of China's most stunning natural beauties and have inspired innumerable paintings, poetry, and other works of art.

Visitors to the Yellow Mountains have the option of hiking along trails that provide breathtaking views of the surrounding area or riding a cable car to the mountain's summit for expansive views. There are several hot springs and other natural attractions in the vicinity.

National Park of Jiuzhaigou:

A wildlife preserve called Jiuzhaigou National Park may be found in the Chinese province of Sichuan. It is renowned for its waterfalls, crystal-clear lakes, and vivid greenery, which combine to form an exquisite natural setting. Other endangered species found in the park include giant pandas, golden monkeys, and snow leopards.

The various features of Jiuzhaigou National Park can be explored by taking a scenic bus tour or hiking along paths that provide breathtaking views of the surrounding area. Additionally, the region is well-known for its Tibetan customs and culture, and visitors can partake in native cuisine, music, and dance while they are there.

The Five Flower Lake, which is renowned for its stunning blue waters and vibrant algae, and the Nuorilang Waterfall, one of the biggest waterfalls in China, are two of Jiuzhaigou National Park's most well-liked attractions. The Shuzheng and Zharu valleys, which are renowned for their woods and mountain splendor, are also accessible to tourists.

Jiuzhaigou National Park's tourists can learn about the history and culture of the region in addition to its natural beauty by visiting nearby Tibetan settlements. Visitors can observe traditional architecture, attire, and rituals while getting an insight into daily Tibetan life in these communities.

Travelers can choose from a wide variety of experiences at China's top ten attractions. There is something for everyone to enjoy in this huge and intriguing country, from the ancient history of the Great Wall and the Forbidden City to the natural wonders of the Yellow Mountains and Jiuzhaigou National Park.

Chapter 2:Food and Drink

China is renowned for its rich and varied cuisine, which includes a wide range of regional cuisines, well-known meals, and snacks, street food, night markets, as well as alcoholic beverages, and tea culture. Each of these subjects will be thoroughly discussed in this post.

Chinese Regional Cuisines

Due to its size, varied geography, and lengthy history, China has produced a wide variety of regional cuisines. Cantonese, Shandong, Hunan, and Jiangsu regional cuisines are a few of the most well-known in China. Each of these cuisines has its flavor profile and cooking methods, and depending on the climate and agriculture of the region, they frequently use different ingredients.

Sichuan pepper and other aromatic spices are used in Sichuan cuisine to produce its distinctively strong and hot flavors. On the other hand, Cantonese cuisine is renowned for its delicate and light flavors and frequently uses seafood and fresh vegetables. The utilization of seafood and the emphasis on the natural flavor of foods are characteristics of Shandong cuisine. The fiery and powerful flavors of Hunan cuisine, which includes chili peppers and garlic, are well-known. Jiangsu cuisine is renowned for its finesse and refinement and frequently uses sophisticated preparation methods to create delicately crafted delicacies.

Popular foods and treats:

There are many tasty and well-liked dishes and snacks in Chinese cuisine that are enjoyed both at home and in restaurants. Kung Pao chicken, stir-fried noodles, dumplings, hot pot, and Peking duck are a few of the most well-liked dishes. Steamed buns, crisp pancakes, tofu pudding, and spring rolls are some examples of Chinese snacks.

Kung Pao chicken is a hot stir stir-Friedl that frequently goes with rice and contains diced chicken, peanuts, and chili peppers. Another well-liked food is stir-fried noodles, which come in many varieties including chow mein and lo mein. With ingredients like pork, shrimp, and veggies as fillings, dumplings are a mainstay of Chinese cuisine. While Peking Duck Ducks is a well-known dish with crispy skin and soft flesh served with pancakes and a choice of sauces, hot pot is a communal dish that includes heating raw ingredients in a boiling pot of broth at the table.

Night markets and eats on the street:

China is renowned for its thriving night markets and street food scene. Jianbing, a type of savory crepe, baozi, steamed buns with a variety of toppings, and a kind of meat sandwich, are some of the most well-liked street snacks. In many Chinese cities, there are night markets that sell a large selection of snacks, souvenirs, and street cuisine.

China's culture of tea: Chinese culture places a high value on tea, which has a long and illustrious history dating back thousands of years. Green tea, black tea, oolong tea, and white tea are just a few of the well-known varieties of tea that originally came from China. Another significant aspect of Chinese culture is tea ceremonies, which can involve complex rituals and involve serving tea alongside tiny nibbles or desserts.

Wine and spirits made in China:

Although drinking wine is not customary in China, the nation nonetheless enjoys traditional alcoholic beverages. At formal banquets and other events, baijiu, a potent distilled alcohol manufactured from sorghum or rice, is frequently served. A rice wine with a mellow, slightly sweet flavor, huangjiu is produced and fermented for several years.

Dining manners and traditions:

Chinese culture places a high value on proper dining manners, and numerous traditions and conventions must be observed when eating there. For instance, it is common to serve elders and guests first and to eat meals as a family. The main tools used in China are chopsticks, and using them to point or make gestures while eating is frowned upon. Additionally, it's crucial to refrain from slurping or belching while you're eating.

Along with these fundamental etiquette guidelines, particular customs differ on the situation and place. For instance, it's traditional to serve a fish meal during the Chinese New Year to represent wealth and luck for the following year. Before the meal, a toast may also be made in some areas, with the host or special guest leading the way.

Another crucial aspect of dining in formal situations is to dress appropriately and be on time. It is customary to wait for the host to start eating before you eat, and to thank them for their hospitality and the food they served.

Chinese cuisine, wine, spirits, as well as dining manners and traditions. There is plenty to learn about and enjoy in Chinese cuisine and culture, regardless of whether you are a foodie or a culture aficionado.

Chapter 3:Accommodations And Cost

China is a huge country with a wide variety of lodging options to accommodate various travel preferences, budgets, and travel types. Travelers enjoy a wide range of lodging alternatives, from luxurious hotels and boutique guesthouses to affordable hostels.

Hotels and other lodging options in China:

China offers a wide range of lodging options, from pricey hotels to convenient hotels. In China, a few of the most typical forms of lodging are:

Hotels: The range of hotels in China includes low-cost lodgings and upscale, luxurious establishments. China's largest cities are home to a wide range of lodging options, including well-known global hotel brands like Hilton, Marriott, and Sheraton.

Hostels: In China, hostels are a popular option for tourists on a tight budget. They typically have convenient locations and provide standard facilities like free Wi-Fi, common kitchens, and public bathrooms.

Guesthouses: Guesthouses in China frequently offer a more individualized experience than hotels because they are smaller and more intimate. They provide an opportunity to experience the local way of life and are typically run by locals.

Homestays: Living with a Chinese family is a wonderful way to learn about their culture. They typically involve lodging and meals with a local family, who will host you.

Apartment rentals are growing more and more common in China, especially with long-term visitors. With the added convenience of a living area and kitchen, they provide a more independent and adaptable experience.

China's Top Luxury Hotels:

Some of the most opulent hotels in the world, with unmatched amenities and services, can be found in China. A couple of China's top luxury hotels are listed below:

The Ritz-Carlton Shanghai: Situated in the center of the city, The Ritz-Carlton Shanghai provides breathtaking views of the Shanghai skyline. The hotel has a top-notch spa, several dining options, and a rooftop bar.

The Waldorf Astoria Beijing is a luxurious hotel situated in Wangfujing, a charming neighborhood near the Forbidden City. The hotel has a rooftop bar, elegant restaurants, and spa services.

The Mandarin Oriental Guangzhou is a luxury hotel with breathtaking views of the Pearl River that is situated in the city's financial center. The hotel has many dining options, a top-notch spa, and a rooftop pool.

Affordable options

In China, traveling on a tight budget doesn't mean forgoing convenience or luxury. Here are a few places to stay in China that are reasonably priced:

Hostels: For tourists in China on a tight budget, hostels are a terrific choice. They typically have convenient locations and provide standard facilities like free Wi-Fi, common kitchens, and public bathrooms.

Budget Hotels: For tourists on a tight budget, inexpensive hotels are a fantastic choice. At a fraction of the price of luxury hotels, they provide rooms that are tidy and pleasant.

Homestays: Experiencing Chinese culture directly while on a budget is possible with homestays. They typically involve lodging and meals with a local family, who will host you.

Guesthouses and Boutique Hotels:

In China, boutique hotels and guesthouses provide a more individualized and private experience. Here are a few of China's top boutique hotels and inns:

The Temple House Chengdu is a posh boutique hotel that is situated in the center of the city. The hotel has a spa, several dining options, and a rooftop bar.

The PuLi Hotel and Spa Shanghai provides a calm refuge from the busy city and is situated in the Jing'an neighborhood. The hotel has a rooftop bar, elegant restaurants, and spa services.

Staying in Traditional Chinese Courtyard Houses: Experiencing local culture in China through a stay in a traditional Chinese courtyard house is distinctive and genuine. Courtyard dwellings, sometimes referred to as "siheyuan," are typical Chinese residences built around a courtyard. They frequently have elaborate carvings and ornamentation and are constructed of brick or wood.

The opportunity to explore traditional Chinese architecture and design is provided to tourists by the numerous courtyard houses that have been transformed into guesthouses in China. In China, some of the most well-known courtyard house guesthouses are:

Beijing Courtyard offers a traditional courtyard home experience with contemporary conveniences like free Wi-Fi and air conditioning. It is situated in the center of Beijing.

Yangshuo Mountain Retreat: This guesthouse offers breathtaking views of the surrounding mountains and rice terraces and is situated in the picturesque Yangshuo region of China. The rooms are located in conventional courtyard homes and are furnished and decorated with antiques.

Hotels Near Popular Attractions:

The Great Wall and the Terracotta Warriors are only two of the famous tourist destinations in China. Here are a few lodging choices close to some of China's biggest tourist destinations:

The Mutianyu part of the Great Wall is only a short stroll away from The Great Wall Hotel Beijing, which offers breathtaking views of the surrounding mountains and countryside.

Xi'an's Terracotta Warriors Museum Hotel: This hotel, which is only a short stroll from the Terracotta Warriors Museum, combines traditional Chinese design with contemporary conveniences like complimentary Wi-Fi and air conditioning.

The price of lodging:

Depending on the type of lodging, the area, and the season, the cost of lodging in China can vary significantly. The following are some typical price ranges for various accommodations in China:

Hostels: Prices for hostels in China normally range from 50 to 150 yuan ($8 to $24) per night.

Budget lodging: A night at one of China's less expensive lodgings normally costs between 150 and 400 yuan (about $24 and $64).

Luxury Hotels: Depending on the location and features, luxury hotels in China can cost anywhere from 500 to 2,000 yuan (about $80-$320) per night or more.

Boutique Hotels and Guesthouses: Nightly rates for boutique hotels and guesthouses in

China normally range from 500 to 1,500 yuan, or around $80-$240.

Traditional Chinese Courtyard Houses: A night's stay in a traditional Chinese courtyard home might run you anything from 500 to 1,500 yuan (about $80-$240).

There are many possibilities in China, whether you're seeking a nice hotel or an affordable hostel.

Chapter 4:Costs and Budgeting

Travelers can enjoy a range of experiences in China due to its size. China has something for everyone, from its sophisticated cities to its ancient culture. It's critical to comprehend the various charges and accessible budgeting solutions when it comes to traveling in China.

Transport expenses:

Particularly in comparison to Western nations, transportation in China can be reasonably priced. In China, buses, trains, and cabs are the three most widely used types of transportation. The least expensive alternative is a bus, with fares in urban areas ranging from CNY 1 to CNY 5 (USD 0.15 to USD 0.75) for each ride. The cost of a train ticket in China is very reasonable, with short-distance excursions costing as little as CNY 20 (USD 3). In China, prices for taxis start at CNY 10 (USD 1.50) for the first three kilometers and increase by CNY 2.3 (USD 0.35) for each additional kilometer.

Average Food Costs:

Any travel experience should include food, and China is home to some of the world's most delectable cuisines. Depending on the kind of restaurant you go to, the price of meals differs in China. The least expensive choice is street food, with prices per dish ranging from CNY 5 to CNY 20 (USD 0.75 to USD 3). Local eateries are likewise reasonably priced, with entrees starting at about CNY 20 (USD 3). Prices might range from CNY 100 to CNY 500 (USD 15 to USD 75) per person if you're searching for a more upscale eating experience.

Charges for Top Attractions:

Some of the most well-known tourist destinations in the world, such as the Great Wall of China, the Forbidden City, and the Terracotta Warriors, may be found in China.

Prices for admission to these attractions range, with smaller attractions' entrance costs starting at about CNY 40 (USD 6) and larger attractions' entrance fees at about CNY 300 (USD 45). Check before you travel because some attractions might give elders or students discounts.

Purchases and souvenirs:

China is a terrific place to shop and buy souvenirs because of its wide selection of goods and competitive rates. Silk, tea, ceramics, and traditional Chinese attire are all well-liked products. Although there are numerous markets and stores where haggling is accepted, prices for these things vary based on quality and location. Scams should be avoided at all costs, particularly when they include fake goods.

Cheap Travel Advice:

There are various methods to save money in China if you are traveling on a tight budget. Staying in hostels or inexpensive motels, which can cost as little as CNY 50 (USD 7.5) per night, is one of the finest methods to save money. Eating at neighborhood eateries or street food vendors, which serve inexpensive and delectable fare, is another option to save money. Because it is affordable and practical, using public transit is another excellent option to save money. Finally, it's critical to prepare ahead and get tickets because last-minute pricing may be higher.

The price of travel varies in China based on the mode of transportation, the cuisine, the tourist attractions, and the souvenirs you select. However, it is possible to travel to China on a budget and take advantage of everything this incredible nation has to offer with a little preparation and planning.

Chapter 5:7 Days Itinerary

Day 1 in Beijing: The Forbidden City and the Great Wall of China

China's capital, Beijing, is a fascinating city that is rich in culture and history. The Great Wall of China and The Forbidden City are two of the most major and well-known sites in the city. One of the greatest architectural feats in human history is the Great Wall, a system of fortifications constructed along China's northern borders. It was constructed throughout several dynasties, beginning in the 7th century BC and ending with the Ming Dynasty, which was the last to maintain and repair it.

Different segments of the wall are accessible to visitors from various points, but the Badaling section is the busiest. It is the most often visited sector because it is well-maintained and convenient. Hikers can enjoy breathtaking panoramas of the surrounding area as they traverse the wall.

The Forbidden City, which served as the imperial residence of the Ming and Qing dynasties, is the next destination after viewing The Great Wall. From 1420 to 1912, it served as the residence of 24 emperors. Today, it houses a museum that explores the history, culture, and artwork of ancient China. The 72-hectare-sized palace complex contains 980 structures, including halls, palaces, and courtyards.

Strolling through the complex, visitors can take in the magnificent architecture, stunning gardens, and countless cultural artifacts on display. For everyone interested in Chinese history and culture, it is a must-see attraction.

Day 2: Tour of Xi'an and the Terracotta Army

One of China's oldest towns, Xi'an is rich in culture and history and is situated in the country's northwest. Throughout many dynasties, the city served as China's capital and was crucial to the growth of the nation. The Terracotta Army is the most well-known of the city's many attractions.

The Terracotta Army is a group of terracotta statues that show the armies of Qin Shi Huang, the first Emperor of China. To safeguard the emperor in the afterlife, the statues were interred with him around 210–209 BCE. Farmers digging a well in 1974 stumbled upon the collection, which has since grown to become one of China's most popular tourist destinations.

More than 8,000 warriors, 130 chariots, and 670 horses make up the Terracotta Army. They are positioned in combat formation, each soldier sporting a distinctive expression. The bronze chariots and weapons that were interred with the troops are also on display for visitors.

The City Wall, the Muslim Quarter, and the Big Wild Goose Pagoda are just a few of the various attractions in Xi'an that are not limited to the Terracotta Army. Visitors can cycle or walk on top of the City Wall, one of China's best-preserved historic fortifications, to take in the expansive views of the city. The Muslim Quarter is a bustling neighborhood with street food vendors, gift shops, and historic buildings. A Buddhist pagoda constructed in the Tang Dynasty, the Big Wild Goose Pagoda is a representation of the city's rich heritage and culture.

Day 3: Yangshuo and sail along the Li River

South China's Guilin is renowned for its spectacular natural beauty. The city is surrounded by karst mountains, flowing rivers, and lush vegetation, making it a well-liked vacation spot for those who enjoy being in nature. A trip on the Li River is among the best ways to appreciate Guilin's splendor.

The Li River, which runs 437 kilometers from Guilin to Yangshuo, is renowned for its breathtaking scenery. Visitors may unwind and take in the sights of the imposing karst mountains, tranquil towns, and fishermen on bamboo rafts while on the voyage. The four to five-hour trip is a fantastic experience that highlights Guilin's beauty.

Visitors can wander through Yangshuo's lovely streets and lanes, which are dotted with gift shops, eateries, and cafes, once they arrive. Outdoor sports including cycling, rock climbing, and hiking are very popular in Yangshuo. A bamboo raft ride on the Yulong River, a tributary of the Li River, allows visitors to soak in the tranquil and beautiful scenery.

Day 4: Giant Pandas and Sichuan Food in Chengdu

The southwestern Chinese city of Chengdu is renowned for its enormous pandas, fiery Sichuan food, and vivacious culture. The Chengdu Research Base of Giant Panda Breeding is the most well-known of the city's many attractions.

Giant panda breeding and conservation are the main goals of the research base, a nonprofit organization. In addition to learning about the pandas' habits, food, and conservation activities, visitors can observe the animals in their natural environment. Over 100 pandas, including infants, young animals, and adults, are housed at the site. The pandas' care can also be assisted by visitors through a volunteer initiative.

Visitors can try the renowned Sichuan food, which is renowned for its potent flavors and spicy taste, after seeing the pandas. One of China's eight regional cuisines, Sichuan cuisine is distinguished by the addition of Sichuan peppercorns, chili peppers, and garlic. Hot pots, kung pao chicken, mapo tofu, and dan noodles are some of the popular foods. In Chengdu, visitors may find delectable meals in every nook and cranny of the city.

Day 5: Jokhang Temple and the Potala Palace in Lhasa

Tibet's Lhasa is renowned for its vibrant Tibetan culture, exquisite monasteries, and breathtaking scenery. One of the highest cities in the world, the city is located at a height of 3,656 meters. The Potala Palace and Jokhang Temple are the two most well-known among the city's many attractions.

The Dalai Lama once lived at the Potala Palace, a UNESCO World Heritage Site. It has two principal palaces, the Red Palace and the White Palace, and was constructed in the seventh century. The palace is renowned for its magnificent gardens, spectacular architecture, and extensive history. Visitors can visit the various chambers and halls and discover the significance of the palace in Tibetan culture and religion.

Another significant Lhasa attraction is the Jokhang Temple, which is regarded as Tibet's most sacred temple. It was constructed in the seventh century and is renowned for both its exquisite exterior and internal design. Numerous Buddha sculptures, prayer wheels, and other sacred relics are kept in the temple. Another unique cultural experience is seeing the villagers perform their daily rituals and prayers.

Visitors can also tour Barkhor Street, a bustling street lined with stores selling traditional Tibetan trinkets, handicrafts, and food, in addition to the Potala Palace and Jokhang Temple.

Day 6: Shanghai City Tour and The Bund

One of China's most contemporary and international cities is Shanghai, which is situated in the country's east. The city is renowned for its breathtaking skyline, iconic sites, and dynamic culture. Shanghai's most well-known tourist destination is

One of the most well-liked tourist attractions in Shanghai is The Bund, a waterfront promenade along the Huangpu River. The promenade is home to numerous historic structures, including the Peace Hotel and the Customs House, and it showcases a variety of architectural styles, including Gothic, Baroque, and Art Deco. Visitors can wander along the promenade and take in the breathtaking views of the river and the city skyline.

Visitors can explore The Bund in addition to other well-known Shanghai sites like the Oriental Pearl Tower, the Shanghai World

Financial Center, and the Shanghai Tower. The Oriental Pearl Tower is a TV tower in Pudong that is renowned for both its unique design and observation deck, which provides sweeping city views. Two of the world's tallest structures, the Shanghai World Financial Center and the Shanghai Tower, provide breathtaking city vistas from their observation decks.

The Old City of Shanghai, a historic district with traditional Chinese buildings, temples, and markets, is another area that tourists can explore. The Yuyuan Garden, a stunning classical Chinese garden constructed in the 16th century, is located in the Old City. In addition, there is the Taoist temple known as the City God Temple, which is devoted to the God of the City.

Day 7: The Yellow Mountains and hot springs in Huangshan

East China's Huangshan is renowned for its breathtaking natural environment, which includes the Yellow Mountains and hot springs. The Yellow Mountains are well-known for their sharp peaks, pine forests, and breathtaking vistas and are a UNESCO World Heritage Site. Visitors can spend a day exploring the many peaks and valleys thanks to the mountains' extensive network of hiking routes and cable cars.

Visitors can unwind and unwind at one of the many hot springs in the region after visiting the Yellow Mountains. The hot springs are a well-liked tourist destination for both locals and visitors because of their well-known medicinal benefits. While relaxing in the hot springs, guests may take in the stunning mountain views in the area.

In addition to the Yellow Mountains and hot springs, tourists can see nearby historic settlements like Hongcun and Xidi. These villages have been conserved as UNESCO World Heritage Sites and are well-known for their traditional Chinese architecture. Visitors can stroll through the winding lanes and alleyways and take in the stunning structures and courtyards.

This seven-day itinerary provides a wide variety of activities and sights, from the historical sites in Beijing and Xi'an to the scenic splendor of Guilin and Huangshan. Visitors will have the opportunity to travel to several parts of China and discover more about the history, culture, and traditions of this enormously diverse nation.

Chapter 6:Getting Around

Travel by air in China:

One of the busiest and largest air transportation networks in the world is found in China. China has more than 200 airports, which offer domestic and international travel options. The majority of the nation's major cities are served by airports, with Beijing Capital International Airport and Shanghai Pudong International Airport serving as the two busiest hubs. Air China, China Eastern, China Southern, and Hainan Airlines are some of the domestic airlines in China.

It's recommended to purchase your tickets in advance if you intend to travel by plane in China, especially if you're doing so during a busy time of year. Additionally, you must get to the airport early to provide time for security screenings and other processes. It's important to bear this in mind when arranging your travel arrangements because

Chinese airports may be highly busy and flights are frequently delayed or canceled.

Rail transportation and fast trains:

The world's largest high-speed rail system, which includes trains capable of 300 kph travel, is found in China. China's high-speed rail network connects the majority of its major cities and tourism hotspots, giving it an easy and effective means of getting about the country. Beijing to Shanghai, Shanghai to Hangzhou, and Guangzhou to Hong Kong are a few of the most well-traveled routes.

It is best to purchase your tickets in advance to guarantee availability if you intend to take a high-speed train in China. Either online or at the railway station is acceptable, though buying tickets online can be more practical if you don't know Chinese. Additionally, you must arrive early at the station to allow for security checks and other processes.

Public transit in significant cities:

Buses, subways, and trams are all part of a well-developed public transit network in the majority of China's main cities. Numerous lines that connect different areas of the city make up the enormous subway systems in major cities, such as Beijing and Shanghai. In Chinese cities, public transit is typically both convenient and economical, and it's frequently the best option to escape the gridlock.

It is imperative to have a map of the system and be familiar with the routes and schedules if you intend to use public transportation in China. Additionally, it's critical to be ready for busy areas, especially during rush hour.

Private drivers, ride-hailing services, and taxis:
In Chinese cities, taxis are a frequent form of transportation, albeit it might be difficult

to hail one during rush hour. In addition to becoming common, ride-hailing services like Didi Chuxing are frequently more practical than taxis. However, using ride-hailing services requires prudence because there have been allegations of safety concerns, particularly for female passengers.

Make sure they are licensed and insured if you intend to utilize a private driver. To avoid any misunderstandings, it is also critical to have an agreement on the price before leaving on your journey.

Tips for domestic travel

It's crucial to always have your passport with you if you intend to travel throughout China. When purchasing rail or plane tickets or checking into hotels, you might need to present it. It's also crucial to respect regional traditions and customs and to be ready for cultural variances.

It's advisable to reserve your lodging and transportation well in advance if you're traveling during the busiest time of year. It's also critical to anticipate crowds and exercise patience while standing in line or traversing busy spaces.

Overcoming linguistic obstacles

Although many people in bigger cities understand English, Chinese is the official language of China, so it's important to be ready for language hurdles, especially when visiting more rural areas. Before your trip, it's a good idea to brush up on some fundamental Chinese words, like greetings and idioms for ordering meals and using the bus. Additionally useful for communication is carrying a phrasebook or having a translation app on your phone.

It's helpful to have your destination written down in Chinese characters or to show the conductor or driver a photo of it on your phone when utilizing public transportation.

This might help you prevent misunderstandings and guarantee that you reach your intended location.

It's helpful to have a photo or description of the dish you desire when ordering food because English-language menus aren't always available. Additionally, it's critical to inform the server in detail of any dietary restrictions or allergies you may have.

It can be thrilling and educational to travel in China, but it's important to be ready and knowledgeable about the various modes of transportation and cultural differences. You may overcome linguistic challenges and take advantage of all that China has to offer by making plans, exercising patience, and respecting local traditions.

Chapter 7:Culture and History

Chinese Dynasties & History:

China has a more than 5,000-year-long history that is both rich and diverse. Its past is divided into several dynasties, each with distinctive traits and accomplishments. The Xia Dynasty, which ruled from 2100 BC to 1600 BC, was the first dynasty. The Shang Dynasty (1600 BC–1046 BC), noted for its bronze metalworking and oracle bone writings, came after it.

The Zhou Dynasty, which lasted from 1046 BC to 256 BC, was divided into two phases: the Western Zhou (1046 BC–771 BC) and the Eastern Zhou (770 BC–256 BC). The Spring and Autumn period (770 BC-476 BC) and the Warring Nations period (475 BC-221 BC), when China was divided into several independent nations, were further divisions of the Eastern Zhou.

China was originally unified under the Qin Dynasty (221 BC–206 BC), which is also renowned for building the Great Wall of China, the Terracotta Army, and its legalist philosophy. The Han Dynasty (206 BC–220 AD), a time of enormous affluence and cultural growth, came after it. Another era of cultural and economic success was the Tang Dynasty (618 AD–907 AD), which is frequently referred to as China's "golden age."

Printing, gunpowder, and paper money were among the technological advances made during the Song Dynasty (960–1279 AD). As the first non-native ruler of China, Kublai Khan established the Yuan Dynasty (1271 AD–1368 AD). The Ming Dynasty (1368–1644) is renowned for the Forbidden City's construction as well as its economic expansion.

The Qing Dynasty (1644 AD–1912 AD), which was established by the Manchu people, was the final dynasty. During this time, China underwent modernization and industrialization as well as substantial engagement with the West.

Chinese traditional arts and Crafts:

Chinese traditional arts and crafts have a lengthy and rich history that represents the culture and values of the nation. Calligraphy, painting, ceramics, silk stitching, paper cutting, and seal carving are a few of the most well-known artistic disciplines.

The practice of writing Chinese characters with a brush and ink is known as Chinese calligraphy. It is highly regarded in Chinese culture and is frequently used as a meditation technique. Chinese painting, which uses a brush and ink to create landscapes, flowers, and animals, is another highly esteemed art genre.

China has a long history with ceramics, which are highly prized for their artistry and beauty. Porcelain, stoneware, and earthenware are some of the most well-known varieties of Chinese ceramics. Another exquisite skill is silk embroidery, which includes utilizing silk thread to produce complex patterns on fabric.

Paper cutting, a well-known folk art, entails chopping elaborate designs from paper. It has a strong symbolic value and is frequently utilized in Chinese celebrations. The craft of cutting seals out of stone or other materials is known as seal carving. Chinese people sign documents with seals, which are highly prized for their artistic and symbolic importance.

Festivals and performing arts:

Chinese festivals and performing arts play a significant role in the tradition and culture of the nation. Opera, dance, and music are traditional forms of Chinese performance art. Using music, dance, and acrobatics, Chinese opera is a highly stylized type of theater. Because of its cultural importance, it has a lengthy history in China and is highly prized.

Chinese traditional dance encompasses a range of genres, such as folk dance, classical dance, and modern dance. Chinese dance is extremely symbolic and frequently conveys stories through its movements, which stand in for particular concepts or feelings.

The pipa, erhu, and guzheng are just a few of the many instruments used in the long-established genre of Chinese music. In traditional Chinese opera and dance performances, traditional Chinese music is frequently played.

Chinese festivals play a significant role in the customs and culture of the nation. The Chinese New Year, the Lantern Festival, the Dragon Boat Festival, and the Mid-Autumn Festival are a few of the most well-known celebrations. Every festival has its particular traditions and rituals, such as consuming mooncakes, lighting lanterns, or competing in dragon boat races.

Chinese spirituality and religion:

There are many different religious and spiritual traditions in China. Buddhism, Taoism, Confucianism, and Christianity are a few of the most well-known religions. One of the most popular religions in China, Buddhism has had a profound impact on Chinese culture and society.

Taoism, a native religion of China, places a strong emphasis on coexisting peacefully with the natural world and the Tao, or path. It has had a big impact on Chinese literature, philosophy, and art. Confucianism is a philosophy that places a strong emphasis on social order, family, and education.

With roots in the seventh century, Christianity is a relatively new religion in

China. Significant numbers of Muslims live in the nation as well, especially in the Xinjiang province.

Cultural customs and etiquette:

The customs and etiquette of Chinese culture are distinctive and may not be the same as those of other cultures. The most significant customs include respecting elders, exchanging presents, and exhibiting modesty and humility.

When dining or attending formal gatherings, it's crucial to address people by their official titles and follow basic manners. In China, it's usual to politely decline gifts and offers before finally accepting them as a mark of respect and humility.

Furthermore, being on time is highly regarded in Chinese society, and it is unprofessional to show up late for appointments or meetings.

Chinese culture in the present day:

Chinese culture nowadays is a fusion of traditional principles and Western ideas. China has rapidly modernized as a result of major economic and social transformations over the past few decades.

Technology, fashion, and popular culture have had a significant impact on contemporary Chinese culture. While still retaining a strong sense of national pride and identity, Chinese adolescents are becoming more interested in Western fashion, music, and entertainment.

The depth of China's past and the breadth of its culture have had a profound effect on the nation and its people. China continues to develop and shape its cultural identity in the contemporary world through the use of modern technologies, popular culture, and traditional arts and crafts.

Chapter 8:Outdoor Adventures

Outdoor excursions offer a great chance to discover nature, push your physical limits, and develop a deeper understanding of the world around us. In this article, we'll look at some of the most popular outdoor activities in China, such as hiking and trekking, mountaineering and rock climbing, kayaking and white-water rafting, cycling and cycling tours, skiing and other winter sports, and visiting national parks and nature preserves.

Chinese hiking and trekking

There are countless chances for hikers and trekkers in China because of its size and diversity. There is something for everyone, from the breathtaking mountains of Tibet and Yunnan to the picturesque trails of Zhangjiajie and Huangshan. The Great Wall of China, Jiuzhaigou National Park, and

Tiger Leaping Gorge are a few of China's well-known hiking and trekking locations.

The Great Wall of China is one of the most well-liked trekking locations in the country. Hikers have access to more than 13,000 miles of wall, which they can explore on a variety of easy to difficult routes. The Jinshanling to Simatai route is well-liked due to its breathtaking scenery and relatively easy terrain.

Another well-liked location for hikers and trekkers is Jiuzhaigou National Park. The park, which is well-known for its stunning lakes and waterfalls, provides a variety of paths, such as the five-lake trail, which leads tourists through some of the most gorgeous areas of the park.

Mountaineering and Rock Climbing

Rock climbing and mountaineering are popular outdoor pursuits in China, where skilled climbers can choose from a variety of difficult routes. Yangshuo, Longdong, and Li Ming are a few of the most well-liked climbing locations in China.

Guangxi Province Is Yangshuo is a charming town renowned for its breathtaking karst peaks and cliffs. With over 300 routes available for climbers of various levels, the area is a well-liked vacation spot.

Another well-known climbing location in China is Longdong, which is situated in Taiwan. The region is well-known for its granite cliffs and provides a variety of routes, ranging from easy to difficult.

Li Ming, which is situated in Yunnan Province, is regarded as one of China's most difficult climbing locations. There are many routes available in the region, including some of the hardest climbs in the nation.

Both kayaking and white-water rafting

White-water rafting and kayaking aficionados will find China to be the ideal location because it is home to some of the most beautiful rivers in the world. The Yangtze River, the Yarlung Tsangpo River, and the Nu River are some of the most well-known rivers in China for rafting and kayaking.

Since it is the longest river in China, the Yangtze provides a variety of white-water rafting and kayaking opportunities, from picturesque floats to heart-pounding rapids.

One of the hardest white-water rivers in the world is the Yarlung Tsangpo River, often called the Brahmaputra River. There are several rafting and kayaking opportunities on the river, including Class V rapids.

White-water rafting and kayaking are increasingly popular activities on the Nu

River in Yunnan Province. The river is renowned for its breathtaking beauty and offers a variety of rapids, from Class III to Class V.

Cycling and Bike Tours

Cycling aficionados should consider visiting China because there are many beautiful routes available all around the nation. The historic city of Xi'an, the Yunnan-Guizhou Plateau, and the Karakoram Highway are some of the most well-liked places to bike and cycle in China.

As a result of the abundance of scenic routes that can be taken through the city's historical streets and the surrounding countryside, the ancient city of Xi'an is a well-liked location for bike and bicycle tours.

Southwest China's Yunnan-Guizhou Plateau is a beautiful region renowned for its beautiful landscapes and extensive cultural history. There are a variety of bicycling and cycling routes through attractive towns, rice terraces, and steep terrain on the plateau, which is home to several ethnic minority groups.

One of the highest international thoroughfares in the world, the Karakoram Highway runs from China to Pakistan. Numerous bike and cycling tours along the roadway provide breathtaking views of snow-covered mountains, deep valleys, and glaciers.

Winter sports and skiing

With numerous ski resorts spread out over the nation, China is quickly gaining popularity as a winter sports destination. Yabuli, Nanshan, and Changbaishan are a few of the well-known ski resorts in China.

One of China's biggest and most well-known ski resorts, Yabuli is situated in Heilongjiang Province. The resort has approximately 30 slopes with a vertical drop of 2,000 feet and offers a variety of skiing and snowboarding activities.

Another well-known ski resort in China is Nanshan, which is situated in Beijing. The resort provides a variety of skiing and snowboarding opportunities, including a half-pipe and a 700-meter terrain park.

Jilin Province's Changbaishan is a picturesque place renowned for its breathtaking natural beauty and abundance of species. With more than 40 lines and a vertical drop of 3,200 feet, the area offers a variety of skiing and snowboarding activities.

Natural areas and national parks

There are numerous national parks and nature reserves in China, giving tourists the chance to see some of the nation's most breathtaking natural settings. Jiuzhaigou National Park, the Three Gorges National Park, and Zhangjiajie National Forest Park are a few well-known national parks and wildlife preserves in China.

Hunan Province's Zhangjiajie National Forest Park is well-known for its enormous sandstone pillars, which provided the setting for the Avatar movie. A variety of hiking and trekking paths wind across the park's breathtaking surroundings.

Sichuan Province's Jiuzhaigou National Park is renowned for its breathtaking waterfalls and lakes. The famed five-lake circuit is just one of the many hiking and trekking trails that the park has to offer.

Along the Yangtze River, the Three Gorges National Park is renowned for its breathtaking natural beauty and extensive cultural history. Numerous activities, such as hiking, boating, and sightseeing, are available in the park.

For people who enjoy outdoor exploration, China has a wide range of adventure activities. There is something for everyone to enjoy, from hiking and trekking to rock climbing and mountaineering, white-water rafting and kayaking to biking and cycling tours, skiing and winter sports to national parks and natural reserves. Therefore, gather your supplies and set out to discover all that China has to offer.

Chapter 9:Shopping and Souvenirs

Whether they are traveling or just looking to buy something new, many individuals like going shopping. Various retail areas in major cities all around the world cater to different tastes and price ranges. There is something for everyone, from upscale boutiques to flea markets.

Major City Shopping Districts:

There are distinctive shopping areas in many large cities that are known for particular types of retailers or goods. For instance, Fifth Avenue in New York City is renowned for its upscale designer stores and opulent boutiques. While Shibuya is well-known for its hip fashion retailers, Ginza in Tokyo is famed for its high-end shopping. The Champs-Élysées is a well-known shopping avenue in Paris, while the Marais is well-known for its chic boutiques and antique stores.

Popular gifts and souvenirs:

Many people enjoy bringing home gifts or keepsakes for themselves or their loved ones when they travel. Local handicrafts, food and drink products, apparel, and accessories are a few of the most popular souvenirs and presents. For instance, you can discover exquisite handcrafted goods like silk scarves, pottery, and wood sculptures in Thailand. Delicious food products like pasta, olive oil, and wine are available in Italy, as well as upscale fashion accessories like leather purses.

Street vendors and markets:

Visit regional markets and street vendors as one way to locate distinctive and reasonably priced souvenirs. You may find markets offering everything from fresh vegetables to handcrafted goods in numerous towns all over the world. It's common for street sellers to sell souvenirs, clothing, and jewelry. When dealing with street vendors, it's crucial to be cautious of scams and carefully negotiate rates.

High-end retail and designer brands:

There are many designer brands and upscale stores to select from for people seeking high-end luxury shopping experiences. Chanel, Louis Vuitton, and Gucci are a few of the most well-known designer labels. Paris, Milan, and New York City are just a few of the destinations where one can find luxury shopping opportunities.

Tips for Bargaining and Haggling:

Negotiating and haggling are frequently required while doing business with street sellers or when shopping in markets. However, it's crucial to exercise consideration and courtesy when haggling over rates. To obtain a sense of what a reasonable price is for the item you are interested in, it can be useful to do some research beforehand. It's also crucial to be ready to leave if you can't agree.

Customs and Shipping Rules:

It's critical to be knowledgeable about shipping and customs policies when traveling. To avoid fines or legal repercussions, it is crucial to abide by the rules that some nations have on what can be exported or brought into the country. Customs fees and taxes should also be considered because they might significantly increase the price of your products. It is important to speak with a specialist or conduct some preliminary study if you are uncertain about shipping or customs restrictions.

A fun and rewarding aspect of traveling can be shopping for gifts and souvenirs. There is something for everyone, whether you prefer high-end retail therapy or distinctive regional crafts. When interacting with street vendors, it's critical to be mindful of customs and shipping laws and to carefully haggle over rates.

Chapter 10:Off the Beaten Path in China

With a long history and diverse population, China is a huge and extremely diverse country. While many tourists travel to the big towns and well-known tourist spots, the country's rural areas and countryside also offer a variety of undiscovered jewels, lesser-known sights, and distinctive experiences. This post will discuss some of the top off-the-beaten-track activities China has to offer, including cultural immersion courses, regional celebrations, and more.

Countryside and Rural Experiences:

Visitors to China have the chance to see a side of the nation that is very different from the bustle of the main cities in the rural and agricultural regions. The following are a few of the most rewarding experiences in these places:

Bike Tour the Countryside: Cycling is one of the greatest methods to discover China's rural areas. In many small towns and villages, you can rent a bike and start your adventure. The rural landscapes around Dali in Yunnan, the rice terraces of Longsheng in Guangxi, and Yangshuo in Guangxi Province are some of the most well-known routes.

Visit a Farm in the Countryside: Rice, tea, and fruit are just a few of the numerous crops that are grown on small, family-run farms throughout rural China. Many of these farms provide guests the opportunity to take part in the growing and harvesting of the crops during guided excursions.

Stay in a Traditional Village: Traditional villages that haven't altered much in generations can be found all over rural China. Visitors can partake in local cuisine and experience traditional Chinese culture and architecture in these communities.

Hike in a National Park: Several stunning national parks in China are ideal for exploring and trekking. Jiuzhaigou in Sichuan, Zhangjiajie in Hunan, and Huangshan in Anhui Province are a few of the most well-known parks.

Programs for cultural immersion

Numerous cultural immersion programs are offered all across China for tourists who want a more comprehensive understanding of the country's culture. These programs may include cultural workshops, language lessons, and homestays with neighborhood families. Popular choices comprise:

Learning the Mandarin language is a fantastic method to become more conversant in Chinese culture and to enhance your communication abilities. Numerous language schools across the nation offer beginner-level to advanced Mandarin training.

Workshops in calligraphy: Calligraphy is a significant kind of art in China, and many tourists take calligraphy lessons to learn more about this age-old discipline. These courses are offered in numerous cities and are typically instructed by seasoned calligraphers.

Homestays with Local Families: Spending time with a local family is a wonderful way to get a personal understanding of Chinese culture. Many rural communities provide homestays, which give tourists the chance to learn more about regional cultures and traditions.

Classes in Martial Arts: Tai Chi, Kung Fu, and Wushu are just a few of the martial arts that originated in China. These subjects are taught in several schools across the nation, allowing tourists to study under accomplished experts.

Opportunities to Volunteer:

Giving back to the community and gaining knowledge of Chinese culture is both possible through volunteering. There are numerous volunteer opportunities across the nation, including:

Teaching English: English teachers are needed in many schools across China, and volunteering to do so is a wonderful way to help young people while also getting a taste of Chinese culture.

Environmental Protection: Volunteers are used in many of China's environmental protection programs. Cleaning up parks and beaches, planting trees, and keeping an eye on wildlife populations are a few examples of these programs.

Animal Rescue: China is home to a large number of groups that help injured and abandoned animals. Volunteers can assist with duties including giving animals food and care, walking dogs, and facilitating adoptions.

Community Development: Throughout China, a large number of nonprofit groups work on community development initiatives like constructing schools, enhancing access to clean water, and assisting with relief operations after natural disasters.

Festivals and events held nearby:

Throughout the year, China hosts a variety of distinctive festivals and festivities, from ancient religious holidays to contemporary cultural events. The following festivals and events are among the most well-liked:

Chinese New Year is the most significant festival in China and is often referred to as the Spring Festival. It is observed in late January or the beginning of February and is a time for gatherings with family, fireworks, and food.

Lantern Festival: The Lantern Festival, which marks the conclusion of the Spring Festival, takes place on the fifteenth day of the Lunar New Year. It is a time for eating sweet glutinous rice balls and burning lanterns.

Dragon Boat Festival: Held every June, the Dragon Boat Festival honors the legacy of the legendary Chinese poet Qu Yuan. The festival features zongzi (sticky rice dumplings), dragon boat racing, and other customary events.

Mid-Autumn Festival: The Mid-Autumn Festival honors the harvest and the full moon and is held in September or October. It's a time for enjoying mooncakes, gazing at the moon, and hanging out with loved ones.

Unusual Dining Situations:

With regional delicacies and distinctive dishes to be found all around the nation,

China is home to diversified and delectable cuisine. Among the most distinctive dining occasions are:

Hot Pot: In this common Chinese cuisine, raw meats, veggies, and other ingredients are cooked at the table in a large pot of boiling broth. It is a wonderful way to share a meal with loved ones.

Chinese cuisine is among the greatest in the world when it comes to street food, and there are many delectable and inexpensive options to choose from. Jianbing, a savory crepe, Roujiamo, a sort of Chinese sandwich, and Xiaolongbao, steamed dumplings are a few common street delicacies.

Peking Duck: A popular Beijing delicacy known for roasting a whole duck until the skin is crispy and serving it with thin pancakes, scallions, and sweet bean sauce is known as Peking Duck. Anyone visiting

Beijing who enjoys food should taste this meal.

Small servings of savory and sweet sweets that are steamed, fried, or baked are served in bamboo baskets as part of the famed Cantonese cuisine known as dim sum. It is a wonderful chance to sample many different dishes all at once.

Visitors can experience a broad variety of off-the-beaten-path activities in China, including rural and countryside excursions, cultural immersion programs, volunteer opportunities, participation in regional festivals and events, and exclusive eating choices. China has plenty to offer everyone, whether you want to discover more about Chinese culture, give back to the local population, or just indulge in some delectable cuisine.

Chapter 11: Travel Tips and Resources

The experience of traveling may be exhilarating and transformative. Having some advice and information available is always beneficial, whether you are an experienced traveler or are arranging your first vacation overseas. Travel-related issues will be covered in this article, including helpful Chinese words and language applications, health and safety advice for travelers, travel insurance, emergency services, internet and communication tools, best travel blogs and forums, and sustainable travel.

Apps that speak Chinese and useful phrases

It is usually advantageous to acquire some fundamental language skills if you intend to travel to China or any other place where the

Chinese language is spoken. The following Chinese phrases are helpful:

(n ho) Good morning (xiè xiè) - I appreciate it (Bù Hoo Si) Please excuse me (du bu q). - I apologize (zài jiàn). - Goodbye (qing wèn) - May I ask you something?

To learn Chinese or any other language you might require for your travels, there are numerous language-learning applications accessible. Duolingo, Babbel, Rosetta Stone, and Memrise are a few of the well-known language learning programs.

Travelers' Health and Safety Advice

To protect your safety and well-being while traveling, it is crucial to exercise caution and be well-prepared. Here are some health and safety recommendations for travelers:

Learn about any safety or health problems at your destination by doing some study before you go, such as finding out about local customs, weather patterns, and medical services.

Get immunized: Depending on where you're going, you might need to get immunized against specific diseases. To find out the immunizations you require, speak with your doctor or a travel clinic.

Avoid insect bites: Malaria and dengue fever are two mosquito-borne illnesses that are common in various regions. Wear long sleeves and pants, apply insect repellent, and if necessary, sleep under a mosquito net to protect yourself.

Develop safe eating and drinking practices: Exercise caution when consuming food and drinks in unexpected settings. Consume only bottled water, steer clear of drinks with ice, and only hot, fully cooked food.

Keep your things secure by keeping an eye out for thieves who might target visitors, such as pickpockets. A hotel safe or a money belt are good places to keep your cash, passport, and other valuables.

Emergency Services and Travel Insurance

When you are on the road, especially when visiting a strange nation, travel insurance can give you peace of mind. Numerous situations, including medical crises, trip cancellations or interruptions, lost or stolen luggage, and travel delays, can be covered by travel insurance.

Make sure to carefully study the policy when getting travel insurance to understand what is and is not covered. Restrictions on pre-existing conditions or particular hobbies, such as extreme sports, may be included in some policies.

It's a good idea to have emergency contact information on hand in addition to travel insurance. The phone numbers for the local embassy or consulate as well as those for emergency services like the police, fire, and ambulance could be included in this.

Communication and Internet Services

For many people, staying healthy when traveling is crucial. Here are some internet and communication options to think about when you're on the road:

Wi-Fi: Free Wi-Fi is widely available in hotels, cafes, and public spaces. Password-protect your devices and stay away from using public Wi-Fi to access crucial data.

SIM cards: Purchasing an inexpensive local SIM card might help you stay connected while traveling. Airports and neighborhood shops both sell SIM cards that can be used with unlocked phones. Before making a purchase, be careful to check the prices and service areas.

International roaming may be an alternative if you would rather utilize your phone and plan. However, it can be pricey, so be sure to inquire about costs and alternatives with your provider before leaving.

Messaging applications: Using messaging applications like WhatsApp, WeChat, and Telegram can make it simple to stay in touch with loved ones while on the go. Through Wi-Fi or data, you may use these apps to exchange messages and make audio and video conversations.

Recommended Forums and Blogs for Travel

There are numerous travel blogs and forums that can offer ideas, suggestions, and guidance for your travels. Here are a few forums and travel blogs we suggest:

On its website, Lonely Planet, a well-known publisher of travel guides, provides a plethora of information, including location guides, travel advice, and trip narratives.

Nomadic Matt - Matt Kepnes is a well-known travel writer who offers suggestions and motivation for travelers on a budget.

TripAdvisor - TripAdvisor is a well-known travel discussion board where users may exchange travel tips, rate hotels, restaurants, and attractions, and post their own experiences.

Reddit Travel - A community of travelers can be found in the Reddit Travel thread, where they may exchange travel stories, seek out help, and offer suggestions and advice.

Greener Travel

Travelers who want to have a minimal negative impact on the environment and who want to help out their communities are becoming more and more interested in sustainable travel. Following are some pointers for eco-friendly travel:

Select eco-friendly lodging: Look for hotels and lodges that use eco-friendly recycling, energy, and water conservation techniques.

Reduce your carbon footprint by opting for walking, cycling, or public transportation instead of hiring a car or hailing a cab. By purchasing carbon offsets, you can also reduce your carbon footprint.

Eat at neighborhood eateries, purchase trinkets from nearby markets, and go on excursions with neighborhood tour guides to support the neighborhood economy.

Follow the "leave no trace" maxim and show respect for the traditions and culture of the area. Do not destroy cultural or natural resources or engage in disrespectful or offensive behavior.

Traveling can be a pleasant and interesting experience, but it's crucial to plan and take security measures to protect yourself. Make your journeys more pleasurable and environmentally friendly by using these suggestions and tools.

Printed in Great Britain
by Amazon

24617365R00056